CONTENTS

What is a ramp?

A ramp is a smooth slope, but it is also a simple machine. It does not look like a machine – it has no wires, **levers** or handles. Levers, springs, screws, pulleys and wheels are also simple machines.

It is easier to roll a barrel up a long gentle slope, or ramp, than up a steep slope.

A machine helps you to do work more easily. It is easier to walk up a long sloping ramp, even if it is further, than it is to climb up a steep slope. And it takes less **force** to pull a heavy weight up a ramp than it does to lift the same weight straight up.

SBC

HOW it WORKS

RAMPS AND WEDGES

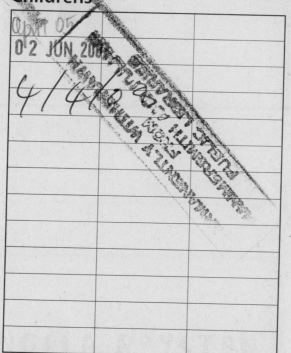

Heinemann
LIBRARY

www.heinemann.co.uk.
Visit our website to find out more information about Heinemann Library books

To order:
☎ Phone ++44 (0)1865 888066
🖹 Send a fax to ++44 (0)1865 314091
🖥 Visit the Heinemann Bookshop at www.heinemann.co.uk to browse our catalogue and order online.

First published in Great Britain by Heinemann Library,
Halley Court, Jordan Hill, Oxford OX2 8EJ,
a division of Reed Educational and Professional Publishing Ltd.
Heinemann is a registered trademark of Reed Educational & Professional Publishing Limited.

OXFORD MELBOURNE AUCKLAND
JOHANNESBURG BLANTYRE GABORONE
IBADAN PORTSMOUTH NH (USA) CHICAGO

Designed by Visual Image
Illustrations by Barry Atkinson
Originated by Dot Gradations
Printed in Hong Kong/China

ISBN 0 431 01754 9 (paperback)

05 04 03 02 01
10 9 8 7 6 5 4 3 2 1

ISBN 0 431 01747 6 (hardback)

05 04 03 02 01
10 9 8 7 6 5 4 3 2

British Library Cataloguing in Publication Data

Royston, Angela
 Ramps and wedges. - (How it works)
 1.Inclined planes - Juvenile literature
 I.Title
 621.8'11

Acknowledgements

The Publishers would like to thank the following for permission to reproduce photographs: Cephas: Mick Rock p4; Corbis: Kevin Fleming p7; Photodisk: p24; Heinemann: Trevor Clifford pp12, 17, 18, 19, 20, 21, 28, 29; John Walmsley: 16; Robert Harding Picture Library: Peter Langone p6; Sue Cunningham Photographic: p15; Sylvia Corday Photo Library: Humphrey Evans p23; Telegraph Colour Library: Robert Clare p5; F McKinney p10, Scott Markewitz p11; Tony Stone Images: Chris Speedle p13

Cover photograph reproduced with permission of Science Photo Library.

The Publishers would like to thank Anthony Mirams for his help and advice with the text and Jo Brooker for making the models on p28-9.

Every effort has been made to contact copyright holders of any material reproduced in this book. Any omissions will be rectified in subsequent printings if notice is given to the Publisher.

Any words appearing in the text in bold, **like this**, are explained in the Glossary.

Try this!

Test a ramp. Make a slope with a board. Tie a piece of string around a heavy dictionary. Use one finger to test which is easier: pulling the dictionary up the slope, or lifting it straight up into the air.

Many big buildings have a short flight of stairs up to the front door. People in wheelchairs can only get in and out of the building if there is a ramp.

Wheels and ramps

A wheel is a simple machine that makes moving things easier. But you cannot wheel something up a flight of stairs. Multi-storey carparks use ramps so that cars can drive from one level to another. Libraries, hospitals and many other places have ramps for people in wheelchairs and pushchairs. This book shows how ramps work and how they are used.

Slopes and slides

Do you like to slide into a swimming pool? The slope lets you drop more slowly than if you jumped in.

Slopes and ramps also make going down easier too. When you slip down the slide in the park, you travel a longer distance than you did climbing up the steps.

What can you do to make yourself slide more slowly? One way is to push your arms or legs against the side of the slide. The more you rub against the slide the more it slows you down. The rubbing is called **friction**.

Jump slides

Water skiers and snow skiers use ramps to jump into the air. The skier slides up the ramp so fast, she keeps on moving after she has left the ramp. The ramp lifts her upwards and forwards. Some skiers jump so high, they can perform acrobatic twists and somersaults in the air before they land.

This water skier is using a ramp to jump high above the water. Expert water skiers can jump over the water as far as half the length of a football pitch.

Think about it!

When you use a slide to go into the swimming pool, do you go faster if you sit up, or if you lean back? What do you think makes the difference?

Building the pyramids

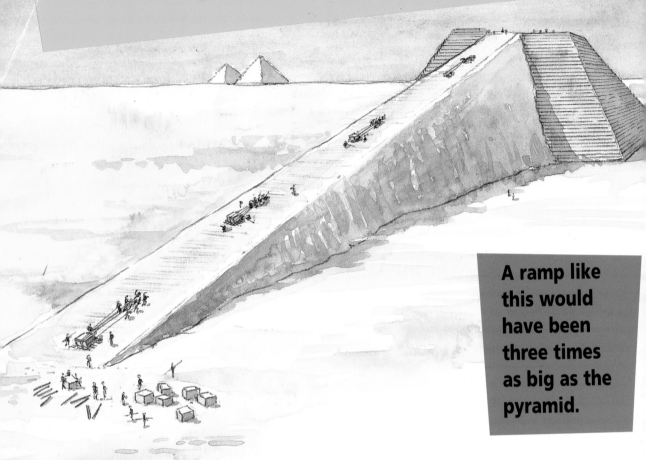

A ramp like this would have been three times as big as the pyramid.

The ramp was one of the earliest simple machines to be invented. The Ancient Egyptians built huge **pyramids** made of very large blocks of stones. The stone blocks were lifted into place without the help of lorries, cranes or even horses.

Archaeologists think that people-power alone, using just a few ramps and **rollers**, lifted the 2.5-tonne stones. It does not seem likely that one long ramp was used. Instead, the ramp was probably built around the pyramid, joining one level to the next, like the ramp in a multi-storey carpark.

Think about it!

Do you think the Egyptians made their ramps from mud or sand? What would have been the advantages and disadvantages of sand? If you were building a ramp to construct a huge stone pyramid, what material would you use for your ramp?

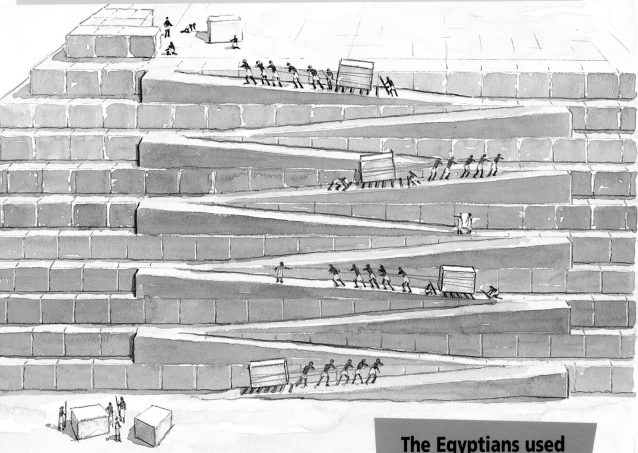

Sledges and rollers

The Ancient Egyptians used other simple machines. They probably **levered** each block onto a sledge. Archaeologists think they might have used tree trunks as rollers to make it easier to pull the sledges.

The Egyptians used gangs of slaves to build the pyramids. Thousands of men probably worked for 20 years to finish the job.

Zig-zag journeys

Many mountain roads make climbing easier by using a zig-zag path. The zig-zag spreads the climbing out over a longer distance.

It is hard work climbing straight up a steep mountain slope. Following a **zig-zag** path makes the distance of the climb longer, but less steep.

Most cars cannot climb very steep hills either. Engineers built mountain roads so that they zig-zag up the slope. This makes the road easier and safer to drive up and down. The bends at the ends of each zig-zag are sometimes very tight. The road almost turns in a full circle.

Make it work!

Draw a zig-zag path from the top to the bottom of a sheet of paper. Measure how long it is. Now draw a straight line from the top to the bottom of the page and measure it. How much longer is the zig-zag path than the straight path?

There is so little friction between the skis and the snow that a skier can move very fast, even when they take a zig-zag path.

Skiing downhill

A zig-zag path makes going down hill easier too. Skiers often zig-zag down steep snow slopes. It helps them control their speed and come down more slowly. If they skied straight down a steep slope, they might lose control and fall.

What is a wedge?

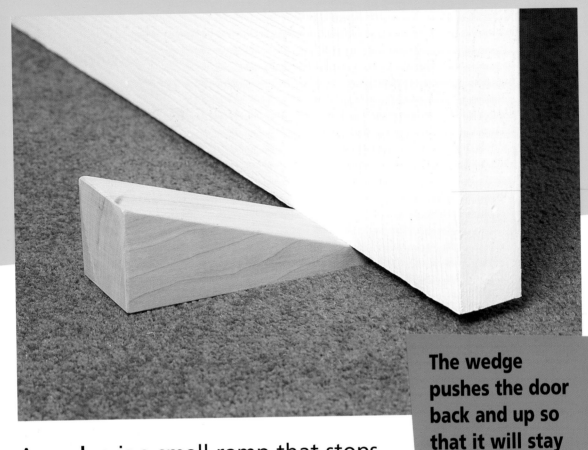

The wedge pushes the door back and up so that it will stay open.

A **wedge** is a small ramp that stops heavy things from moving. For example, if you place a small, narrow wedge under a door, it will jam the door open. The thin edge of the wedge fits easily under the door, but as you try to close it, the door moves up the slope until it jams.

As the door pushes against the wedge, it increases the amount of **friction** between the wedge and the floor and stops the wedge slipping. The rougher the floor, the better the wedge will work. A carpet will produce more friction than a smooth vinyl floor.

The slope of the starting block pushes the sprinter up and forwards.

Starting blocks

In a race, **sprinters** use wedge-shaped blocks to push them off to a fast start. As the sprinters push their feet down and back, the angle of the blocks pushes them up and forwards.

Powerful wedges

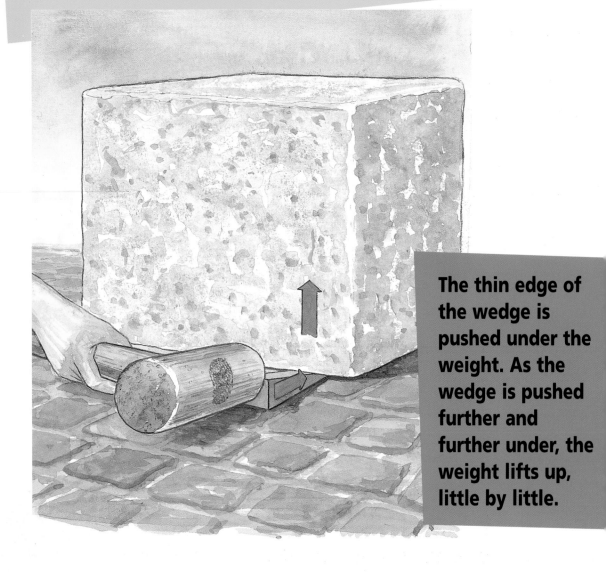

The thin edge of the wedge is pushed under the weight. As the wedge is pushed further and further under, the weight lifts up, little by little.

A small **wedge** can be used to lift a heavy weight. It takes less **force** than lifting the weight straight up, because the tip of the wedge moves a long way to lift the weight just a little. The wedge changes the direction of the force – as the wedge is pushed forward, it lifts the weight up. Wedges are often used to lift a heavy weight just enough to get a **lever** underneath it.

Try this!

Find a chair that does not sit evenly on the floor, but rocks slightly as you move your weight. Fold a piece of paper, two, three or four times. Use it to wedge the chair steady. Which part of the paper will you put under the leg of the chair – the folded edge or the loose edges?

Splitting a stone

Wedges are used to split chunks of stone, but the wedges cannot be used on their own. Instead, the stone-cutter hits the thick end of the wedge with a heavy hammer. The thin edge cracks the stone. He hits in another wedge next to it to make the crack larger. As he hits first one wedge and then the other, the wedges are forced into the crack making it deeper. Eventually the stone splits into two.

The force of the hammer hitting the wide end of the wedge becomes an even stronger force at the sharp end.

Sharp wedges

The wood cutter lifts the heavy head of the axe and lets it fall onto the log. All the weight of the fall is concentrated onto the sharp edge of the blade. Be careful: sharp blades are dangerous.

The **blade** of the axe is a thin, sharp **wedge**. As the blade hits the wood, all the **force** is concentrated on the sharp edge of the blade. Bit by bit the blade is pushed into the wood. As the thin edge of the blade moves in, the thicker end of the blade makes the split in the wood wider. Eventually the block of wood breaks into two parts.

Even a blunt knife will easily cut into an apple. The force on the handle is concentrated on the edge of the blade.

Knives

The blade of the knife is a wedge too. As you move the knife back and forwards, the blade cuts into the apple. As the sharp edge of the blade moves down, the thicker part of the blade pushes the sides of the cut apart.

Think about it!

The first axes were made of sharp pieces of hard, strong stone such as flint. Early people used one stone as a wedge to chip the edge of a piece of flint to give it a sharp blade. The wedge-shaped flint was then tied to a wooden handle to make an axe.

Saws

A saw is a long knife with a **serrated**, or **zig-zag**, **blade**. Some kitchen knives have a serrated edge too. They are particularly useful for cutting fruit and vegetables. The whole blade is **wedge**-shaped, like an ordinary knife, and the blade itself is split into many smaller wedges.

Different parts of the blade point in different directions. The sharp points dig into the vegetable or wood and the sloping edges widen the cuts as the blade moves backwards and forwards. A serrated blade has a longer sharp edge than an ordinary blade.

18

Hedge-trimmer

The **hedge-trimmer** has many wedge-shaped blades that move from side to side. As gaps open up between the blades, the stems of the hedge are caught between them. As the blades move across each other, they slice the stems.

An electric trimmer has two serrated blades which cut through twigs and thin branches easily.

Think about it!

Danger! Saws, knives and axes are very sharp and can be dangerous. Be careful with knives and keep a safe distance away from anyone using an axe or a saw. Electrical knives, trimmers and cutters are fast and powerful. Only adults should use them.

Scissors and cutters

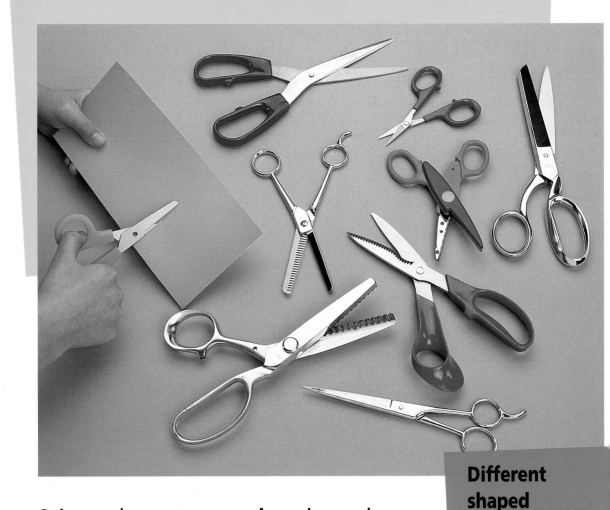

Different shaped scissors are used to cut different things.

Scissors have two **wedge**-shaped **blades** that work together. When you open the scissors, the blades make a 'V' shape. The blades trap the edge of the paper in the point of the 'V' and cut from both sides. As you close the handles, the blades **force** the paper apart.

Scissors produce a strong force at the point where they cut, and the long blades allow you to control the cut. You can cut a straight edge, or you can cut around a wavy line.

Try this!

Draw a large letter 'S' on a sheet of paper. Use a pair of scissors to cut around the shape. First, hold the paper still and move the scissors around the shape. Then hold the scissors steady and move the paper as you cut. Which way is better?

Secateurs are used to prune roses and other garden shrubs. The word 'secateur' means 'cutter' in French.

Secateurs

Secateurs are used for pruning shrubs in the garden. They cut through twigs and thin branches. They have short, curved blades and handles for the gardener to hold. The handles move a long way to come together and the blades a short way to come together. This produces a strong cutting force between the blades.

Spades, diggers and ploughs

A spade is one of the simplest digging tools. Mechanical diggers use motors and specially shaped blades to break up different kinds of ground.

Gardeners use a spade with a **wedge**-shaped **blade** and a long handle to dig into the soil. The gardener often puts a foot on top of the blade and uses his or her weight to push the blade into the soil with more force. The long handle is a **lever** which makes it easier to lift the chunk of soil and turn it over.

Think about it!

Gardeners use trowels, hoes and forks to do different jobs in the garden. Find out what each is used for. How does the shape of each make it particularly suited to the job it does?

A plough has sharp, curved blades. The sharp edge of each blade cuts into the soil and the curve turns the soil over.

Mechanical diggers

A mechanical digger is used to break up the surface of the road. It has a narrow wedge-shaped blade. The motor makes the blade hit the road with many short, sharp bangs.

Other kinds of mechanical diggers include bulldozers and ploughs. A bulldozer has a long sharp blade for cutting into the earth. A plough has many curved blades.

The incredible zip

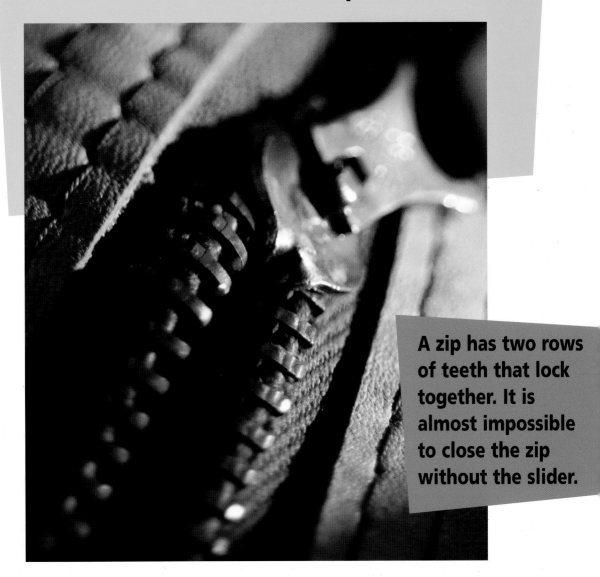

A zip has two rows of teeth that lock together. It is almost impossible to close the zip without the slider.

A zip is a quick and easy way to fasten a coat, but it was only invented just over a hundred years ago. At that time women wore long boots that were fastened with laces hooked around lots of tiny buttons. The zipper was invented as an easier way to do up boots. It is now used to fasten trousers, jackets, cushion covers, bags and many other things. What else do you have that fastens with a zip?

How a zip works

A zip has two rows of teeth that fit together to make a tight seam. The teeth are pushed together and pulled apart by a slider. The slider itself is **wedge**-shaped and inside are three more wedges. When you pull the slider down, a wedge at the top pushes the teeth apart. When you pull the slider up, two wedges at the side push the teeth together.

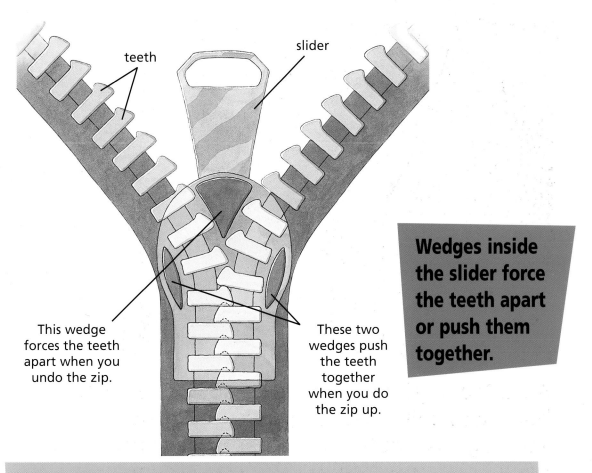

teeth

slider

This wedge forces the teeth apart when you undo the zip.

These two wedges push the teeth together when you do the zip up.

Wedges inside the slider force the teeth apart or push them together.

Think about it!

Why do you think most shoes still use laces or velcro instead of zips? What are the advantages of using zips instead of buttons on clothes?

Lock and key

pins stop barrel
turning

springs to push
pins down

split in pin

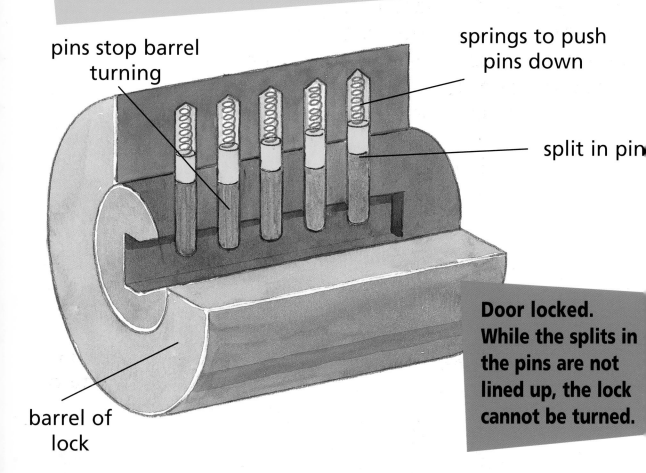

barrel of
lock

**Door locked.
While the splits in
the pins are not
lined up, the lock
cannot be turned.**

Does your front door have a lock with a notched metal key? This kind of lock is often called a Yale lock, after its inventor, Linus Yale. The key is a series of **wedges** which lift five pins inside the lock.

The lock consists of a round barrel in a metal block and five **split pins**. When the door is locked the pins hold the barrel in the lock. The lock can only be turned when the splits in the pins line up along the gap between the barrel and the block.

Opening the lock

Each pin is split at a different height. When you put the notched key into the lock, the notches wedge each pin up so the splits line up. Then the key can be turned to open the door. Each lock has a different combination of split pins, so only the right key will open it. And each notch is roughly 'V' shaped. This allows the key to slide in and out of the lock.

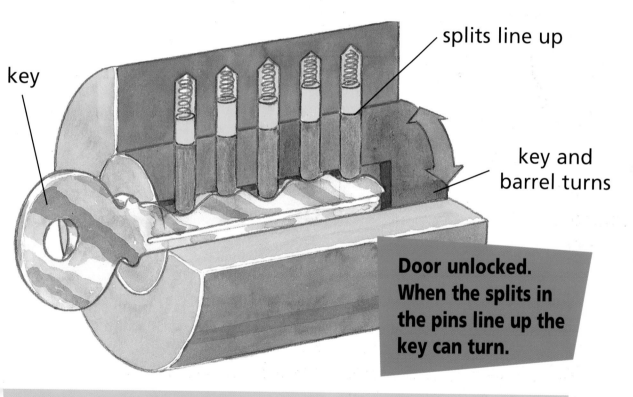

splits line up

key

key and barrel turns

Door unlocked. When the splits in the pins line up the key can turn.

Make it work!

Draw a design for a Yale lock and key. Remember you have to split each pair of pins in a different place. Then you have to draw notches on the key that will make the splits line up. Make sure your key is able to slip in and out of the lock.

Make a zig-zag bottle run

Use empty plastic bottles and cardboard tubes to make a ramp for rolling balls or marbles down.

You will need:

- a flight of stairs with banisters
- 6-12 large empty plastic bottles or cardboard tubes
- scissors
- string
- small balls (such as ping-pong balls) or large marbles

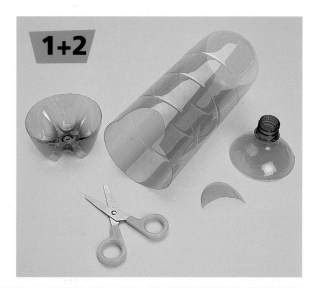

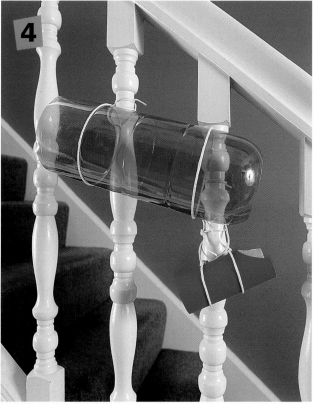

1   Ask an adult to cut a slice off the bottom and top of each bottle.

2   Ask an adult to cut a bite out of one end of each bottle and cardboard tube.

3   Tie the first bottle to the banisters at the top of the stairs. Tie it at an angle so that it slopes down.

4   Position the second bottle so that the hole in the top is underneath the end of the bottle above. Tie the second bottle to the banisters so that it slopes downwards and backwards.

5   Carry on with the next bottle pointing forwards and then the next one downwards or backwards, and so on until you have used all the bottles.

6   Drop a ball into the bottle at the top of the stairs and watch it travel all the way down.

7   Try running model cars down the bottle run. You may have to change the run to make the bottles slope less steeply.

Glossary

blade the sharp, flat cutting part of a knife or other instrument

force a push or pull that makes something move

friction rubbing between two surfaces as one slides over the other

hedge-trimmer tool with many sharp blades used to cut hedges

lever a simple machine which is usually used to lift or balance something

pyramid a three-dimensional shape with a square base and triangular sides. The Egyptians built huge pyramids of stone.

roller a cylinder which rolls

secateurs tool with two short, sharp blades for cutting twigs

serrated with a sharp, zig-zag edge

split pin a pin which is cut into two parts

sprinter an athlete who runs fast races over a short distance

vertically straight up and down

vibrate move backwards and forwards very fast

wedge a triangular-shaped block

zig-zag jagged with many sharp turns from one side to the other

Answers to questions

p7 You slide faster if you lie back. When you lie back, your body is more streamlined. Although more of your body touches the slide, the water reduces the **friction** between the two surfaces. When you sit up, the air catches on your body and slows you down. Also your weight presses on a smaller area of the slide and so increases the friction.

p9 Egyptians probably used earth or mud to build their ramps. Plenty of sand would have been available since the pyramids are built on the edge of the desert, but the sledges and **rollers** would have sunk into sand.

p13 Heavier objects make better **wedges** than lighter objects of the same shape, but even small, light wedges can work. Balls do not make good wedges because there is little friction with the floor and so they roll too easily. It is best to put a wedge at the handle end of the door.

p15 When you fold paper several times, the folds are thicker than the loose edges. So it is better to put the loose edges under the leg.

p21 It should be easier to control the scissors if you hold them steady and move the paper.

p23 A trowel is small with high sides for scooping up small amounts of earth. A hoe has a flat, horizontal blade and a long handle for digging up weeds without having to bend over. A fork has pointed prongs to make it easier to dig into heavy or hard earth.

p25 Shoes use laces or velcro so that they will fit a wider range of feet. You can tie laces tighter if your foot is narrow or leave the laces slacker if your foot is wider. A zip, however, cannot be adjusted. Zips on clothes are quicker to do and undo than buttons.

Index